# History of Britain

# Tudor Family Life

## Jane Shuter

Illustrated by Mark Bergin and James Field

**Heinemann**

Schools Library and Information Service

HISTORY OF BRITAIN – TUDOR FAMILY LIFE
was produced for Heinemann Children's Reference
by Lionheart Books, London.

Editors: Lionel Bender and Peter MacDonald
Designer: Ben White
Editorial Assistant: Madeleine Samuel
Picture Researcher: Jennie Karrach
Media Conversion and Typesetting: Peter MacDonald
Editorial Advisors: Andrew Farrow, Paul Shuter

Production Controller: David Lawrence
Editorial Director: David Riley

First published in Great Britain in 1997 by
Heinemann Educational Publishers, a division of Reed
Educational and Professional Publishing Limited,
Halley Court, Jordan Hill, Oxford OX2 8EJ.

MADRID ATHENS
FLORENCE PRAGUE WARSAW
PORTSMOUTH NH CHICAGO SAO PAULO MEXICO
SINGAPORE TOKYO MELBOURNE AUCKLAND
IBADAN GABORONE JOHANNESBURG KAMPALA NAIROBI

ISBN 0431 057222 Hb    ISBN 0431 057354 Pb

British Library Cataloguing-in-Publication Data.
A catalogue record for this book is available
from the British Library.

Printed in Hong Kong

Acknowledgements
Artwork credits
Mark Bergin: 6-7, 8-9, 10-11, 14-15, 18-19, 20-21.
James Field: 4-5, 12-13, 16-17, 22-23.

Picture credits
Pages 4: Fotomas Index. 5: National Portrait Gallery, London.
6: © Crown Copyright/National Monuments Record Centre.
7: The Royal Collection ©/By Courtesy of Her Majesty the Queen.
8: The Bridgeman Art Library/Longleat House, Wiltshire (part only).
9: The Bridgeman Art Library/Private Collection (part only).
10: The National Trust Photographic Library/John Hammond.
11: Fotomas Index. 12: Fotomas Index. 13: The Bridgeman Art Library/
Christie's, London. 14-15: Fotomas Index. 15: The Bridgeman Art
Library/Burghley House Collection, Lincolnshire. 16: Fotomas Index.
17: By Courtesy of Essex County Record Office. 18: The Bridgeman Art
Library/British Library, London. Add. Ms 24098. (part only). 19: Michael
Holford. 20: The Bridgeman Art Library/Kunsthistorisches Museum,
Vienna. 21: Fotomas Index. 22: The National Trust Photographic
Library/Derrick E. Witty.

Cover illustration: Mark Bergin.
Cover photo: National Portrait Gallery, London.

# PLACES TO VISIT

Here are some Tudor family houses and museums you can visit. Some of them are not open all year round. Your local Tourist Office can tell you about other places in your area.

**Avoncroft Museum of Buildings,** Stoke Heath, Bromsgrove, Hereford and Worcester. Open air museum with houses from all periods, including Tudor.

**Buckland Abbey,** Yelverton, Devon. Home of Sir Francis Drake. A good example of a Tudor family home; also has relics of Drake.

**Burghley House,** Cambridgeshire. Good for everyday noble life. Lots of famous paintings of important people.

**Elizabethan House,** Plymouth, Devon.

**Geoffreye Museum,** London. Rooms from different periods, including a late-Tudor room.

**Hardwick Hall,** Derbyshire. A good example of re-building by the rich. A grand house with furnishings and gardens.

**Hatfield House,** Hatfield, Hertfordshire. A very grand house with famous Tudor paintings. Also has hat, gloves and stockings of Queen Elizabeth I!

**Highland Folk Museum,** Kingussie, Scotland. Good for everyday homes of poor, rural families.

**Ingatestone Hall,** Essex. Held by the Petrie family. Good example of largish country manor house, with lots of family pictures and Tudor furniture.

**Kenilworth Castle,** Warwickshire. The home of Queen Elizabeth I's close admirer, Robert Dudley.

**Knole,** Kent. This huge, rambling Tudor house was once a royal palace. It is surrounded by a vast deer park.

**Museum of London,** London Wall, London. Has a Tudor section, including clothes.

**National Trust Museum of Childhood,** Sudbury Hall, Sudbury, Derbyshire. Also try museums of childhood in your area; many cities have them.

**Paycocke's,** Coggeshall, Essex. An early Tudor merchant's house (around 1500).

**Purse Caundle Manor,** near Sherbourne, Dorset. Interesting small family manor. NOT ALWAYS OPEN, check opening times (01963 250400).

**Stratford-on-Avon,** Warwickshire. Shakespeare's birthplace, Anne Hathaway's cottage, Dr Hall's croft and Mary Arden's house are all in and around Stratford. They give a good picture of ordinary life in a small town and the countryside.

**Tudor Merchant's House,** Quay Hill, Tenby, Wales. An early Tudor town house.

**Victoria and Albert Museum,** London. Has a Tudor section, including panelled room and clothes.

**Whittington Court,** Whittington, near Cheltenham, Gloucestershire. Small manor house. A good example of the family home of a country gentleman. Family possessions. NOT ALWAYS OPEN, check opening times (01242 820218).

# INTRODUCTION

What was family life like during the Tudor period (1485-1603)? That depended on your family. How people lived varied according to how rich they were, and where they lived. The life of a rich family in the countryside was very different from the life of a poor family in a town, for example. Families were a good deal larger than they are now. This is partly because people had more children, and because grandparents were usually part of the family. It is also because the family included other people who lived and worked in the family home.

In Tudor families, each person had their own part to play. In this book, we are going to look at how different members of the family contributed to family life at the time.

# CONTENTS

# WHO WAS IN THE FAMILY?

**Tudor families were organized like Tudor society. In England, the most important person was the monarch, followed by nobles, gentlemen, ordinary people and the poor. The people at each level had different duties – things they had to do for other people. They also had different rights – things they could expect other people to do for them.**

The person in charge of the family was the head of the household. Usually this was a man: everybody had to obey him. In return, he had to look after everyone, from his wife and children to the lowly servants.

◁ **Life on a Tudor farm.** The family are listed in order of importance. Everyone else in the household is a servant.
**1** The head of the house runs the farm. **2** His wife looks after the farmhouse, dairy and gardens. **3** His eldest son helps on the farm until he can set up a farm on his own. **4** This son's wife helps the farmer's wife. **5** and **6** The farmer's daughters learn to run the farmhouse.
**7** The farmer's youngest son helps out.

▽ **Not every family had a home.** This homeless woman and her children are beggars who live on the streets, begging for food.

◁ **The family of Sir Thomas More.** Part of this picture is a copy of a painting made while More was still alive. The new painting was ordered by Thomas More's grandson, in about 1593. He added himself (sitting on the right in a tall hat), his wife and two sons (with ruffs like his around their necks). So the grandson looks older than his father, who is the hatless young man reading a book at the back.

◁ **Most farm work was divided up by sex.** Men worked in the fields, women in the house, yard, garden and dairy. Women helped in the fields at harvest time.

Women grew or made most of the farm food. They fed hens, collected the eggs, milked the cows, made butter, got honey from the beehives and grew vegetables.

The next most important person to the head of the household was his wife. After her came any grown-up relatives who were living with the family. Then came the children. Finally there were the servants, who had their own levels of importance.

Each group of people had to obey the members of the household who were more important than they were. It was also their duty to look after the less important people. The head of the house did not have to obey anyone there. But outside the home he would have to obey the local lord, the king, and God.

The least important servants had to obey everyone. But there was no one less important that they had to look after. They were 'at the bottom of the pile'.

5

# HUSBANDS AND FATHERS

**"God has blessed you with a household. So you must make sure that no one in it does anything to offend God. You must make sure they behave, go to church, keep to their place in the household and work hard," a Tudor preacher, Thomas Becon, told his listeners.**

This quotation makes it sound as if the heads of Tudor households were on constant patrol, watching everyone to see if they made a mistake and punishing them if they did.

In fact, there were good and bad husbands and fathers, just like today. Some of them were strict, and made sure that everyone obeyed the rules. Others were more relaxed. If the work was getting done, they didn't mind if servants made themselves a bit of free time. There were others who were not decisive or strict enough and were largely ignored by their household.

Rich households were the biggest. It was in these households that fathers and husbands were the most likely to insist on order, and on people minding their place. It was, in many ways, the best way to make sure that jobs got done in a household of anything up to 50 people. It also stopped squabbles about who could give orders and who had to obey. In smaller households it was easier to keep things going while letting people work at their own pace.

▷ **A memorial to a husband and wife and their children,** in a church in Shropshire. It was made in 1577.

▷ **Merchants and sailors would often stay in taverns** when they were travelling far from home.

6

The age that men married varied. Rich men often had their marriages arranged by their parents. They would marry at about 21. Other men waited until they could run a household. So craft workers might wait until they were trained and could set up a business on their own. This meant not marrying until they were aged about 30. Not everyone did this. Some people married and lived with their parents or relatives instead.

△ **Henry VIII (centre), his only son, Edward, and his wife, Jane Seymour.** Sons were important to a family. Only male heirs carried on the family name and kept family lands. Sons were most important to kings, to rule the country after them. Henry VIII had six wives. But the only wife he had official pictures like this painted of was Jane, the wife who had his only son.

◁ **This family runs the local tavern.** The father deals with the customers, but all the family lend a hand pouring and serving drinks and clearing up the tables.

# WIVES AND MOTHERS

"She should run the home," John Lyly wrote in a book of advice to Tudor husbands. "Let the house keys hang from her belt – but make sure the purse hangs from yours." This statement puts Tudor women firmly in their place in the family.

▽ **Lady Lettice Knollys,** daughter of one of Elizabeth I's advisors, as painted in about 1585. She is dressed in a ruff and fine clothes to attend the queen's court.

◁ **A picnic at a nobleman's house.** People often ate outside in good weather. Young noblewomen were often sent to be part of another household to learn how to behave. The host family would be paid to look after them.

△ **Lady Tasburgh of Norfolk** with her children. Once they were married, noblewomen were no longer welcome at court. Their husbands went but the women were expected to stay at home and look after the children.

Throughout their lives, women were expected to obey a man – first their father, then their husband. Even so, they were very important to the family. They ran the home. In some noble households this meant giving orders to lots of people.

Even in smaller households, for example those of farmers, there would be children and servants to organize and accounts to keep. Sabine, wife of John Johnson, a wool merchant, had to give a careful account of every penny she spent. Accounts of large households got very complicated, so they were often kept and written up by a manager.

There were women who ran more than just the home. Queen Elizabeth I ran the country. That was because there had not been any royal males to inherit the throne. If there had been, a baby boy would have been chosen to rule instead of her. Elizabeth stressed constantly how like her father she was, how brave she was, how educated she was. How like a man she was, in fact!

What about other women who ran the family? How did they do it? Some had strong personalities and their husbands did not. Some widows inherited their husbands' businesses and did not re-marry. (If they re-married, everything they owned went to their new husband.) Bess of Hardwick married four times, becoming more important each time. She stayed a widow after her fourth husband died, and spent much of her time organizing the building of many grand houses, including Hardwick Hall. Bess ran all the family estates herself.

# Babies and Toddlers

**"For easy growing of the teeth, cover the gums with a mixture of hare's brains, goose fat and honey,"** advised a Tudor childcare book. Growing up in Tudor England was an unpleasant business!

Giving birth was dangerous for the mother and the baby. If there were any complications with the birth, both mother and baby could die. There were no hospitals, no antiseptics for operations, not much medicine to ease pain. But Tudor women kept on having babies. It was their family duty.

If they survived the birth – as many as six out of every ten died at birth – many babies and toddlers were still likely to die. So families needed two or three boys to be sure of one surviving to be an heir. Poor families had just as many babies as rich ones, an average of five. But poor families ended up with fewer toddlers in the house. More poor babies died in the cold, damp, dirty houses. Some babies were abandoned: they either died or were looked after by the local church, which collected money from everyone in the neighbourhood to care for the old, the sick, abandoned babies and orphans.

▷ **Lady Arabella Stuart, aged 23 months, with her doll.** Arabella was related to Bess of Hardwick. Bess was always trying to marry her off, even as a child. The doll that young Arabella is holding would have been very expensive. It was carefully made and dressed in the fashion of the time. Even rich children would have had just a few toys, which they would have to look after very carefully. Poor children would have one hand-made wooden doll.

Babies were swaddled (wrapped in cloths like an Egyptian mummy) as soon as they were born. This kept them still and quiet. Mothers could carry them out to the fields or into the kitchen and know they were safe. The wrappings were supposed be changed regularly, but it was a long, awkward job. It was probably not always done often enough.

△ **This drawing, by the Tudor court painter Hans Holbein,** shows a mother with her children.

◁ **The country house of a rich family.** The father is away, at court. The mother, who may well have been to court as a young girl, is left behind to look after the home. Here she is talking and playing with the children.
Can you find:
• The hobby horse the boy is playing with.
• The early baby walker?

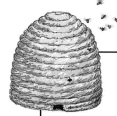

# OLDER CHILDREN

**In Tudor times, children were expected to learn to behave like adults from the earliest possible age. There were several stages to growing up.**

For boys, the first of these was 'breeching'. This was when they stopped wearing frocks like their sister and began wearing breeches. This happened when they were about six. The first important stage for girls and boys was when they were confirmed in church. The earliest age they could do this was at 14. Most children were confirmed by the age of 16. This was also the age when boys could first be called to serve in the army. Most people over 16 were treated by everyone as adults. By that age some of them had been doing adult work for four or five years.

▽ **Harvest time in the country.** There were no machines to help with the harvesting. Everything was done by hand, from cutting the wheat to stacking it in the barn. It took a lot of people a long time and had to be done quickly, in case it rained and the wheat was spoiled. Everyone in the family, including young children, had to help.

▽ **Children had to be quiet and attentive.** In this Tudor drawing the father is explaining the Bible psalms to his family on a Sunday. Even the baby has to listen. There were several reasons for doing this. It taught children about God, which was important. Also, the children were learning to obey their father.

Unless their parents were very rich, children were working, or preparing for work, from about the age of ten. They were often sent to other people's homes for this. Even rich people sent their children to live with other rich people to be taught how to behave at court. Girls were taught to run the house. The boys from families who could afford it went to school then to universities of the Inns of Court (which taught law). This prepared them for working in the government, or running a rich person's lands. Poorer boys went to learn a trade, like shoemaking, carpentry or butchery.

△ **Once they were 'breeched'**, boys were expected to behave like men. This boy is ready for the 'manly' sport of hunting.

▽ **Children in farming families started work at an early age.** They began by helping around the house, as soon as they could walk. From the age of six or so they did easy farm jobs like gleaning (gathering the cut corn) or helping in the dairy. As they got older and stronger, they did harder jobs.

# RELATIVES

**Many households had relatives of the head of the house living there. They might be his parents or younger brothers or sisters with no home of their own. They might be children of relations whose parents had died. Here is one family as an example.**

The picture shows a typical Tudor household at dinner. The head of the house (1) is sitting at the end of the table furthest from the fire. He is a tailor, and makes clothes from a workshop at the front of the house. Sitting on his left is his eldest son (2) who has just finished training as a tailor. His mother died having a second child, which also died soon after birth.

The father married again. His second wife (3) and her two children (4 and 5) are at the near end of the table. Sitting next to the eldest son is the head of the house's nephew (6). Both of the nephew's parents died of fever, so he lives with the family and is learning to be a tailor. Opposite him is another apprentice (7), who is also learning tailoring. This apprentice's sister (8) also works in the household. She is the servant pouring ale. The old lady by the fire (9) is the mother-in-law of the head of the house. Her husband is dead. Next to her is another servant (10), a cousin of the other serving girl. People often tried to find their relatives work in the same house, if they liked working there.

▷ **A tailor's workshop.** The tailor is cutting cloth at his workbench while his apprentices sew the pieces together to make the finished garment.

▽ **The tailor's household at dinner.** There must have been a 'buzz' of conversation with so many people in the room.

▷ **A painting of Anthony, John and William Browne.** The brothers all wear black. The man on the right is too well dressed to be a servant but he has taken off his hat, which shows he is less important than the people he is with. He might be a ward. Wards were noble children whose parents had died. Another family took them in and ran their lands until the wards were adults.

# SERVANTS

In 1545, John Johnson, a rich wool merchant, wrote home to his wife, Sabine: "Master Pratt, the new apprentice, has written to his mother complaining he has not enough to eat or drink. He says everyone says the same." He told her to sack all who said so.

◁ **Apprentices, like the cook's apprentice shown on the right,** could expect to be beaten if they did not do as they were told.

△ **Some Tudor servants.** From left to right: a workman, a dairy maid, a kitchen servant, a washerwoman, a cook's apprentice and a cook.

▽ **A servant in an inn** pours wine for the customers. The servant is less well-dressed than they are.

Servants were badly treated in some households. Apprentices signed a contract with their master saying what their duties would be and what they would get in return. Their payment terms might be phrased as "bed and board" – which could be as little as a shared bedroom and sharing the family meal.

No two servants had exactly the same living and working conditions. Noble families had lots of servants. The most important of these lived better than many gentlemen! But most servants worked in a smaller household, like that of the Johnsons. Many poorer families had just one maid.

Servants were paid varying wages, depending on their jobs. The least important servants were the children who were learning their job – they got no wages but were fed and clothed.

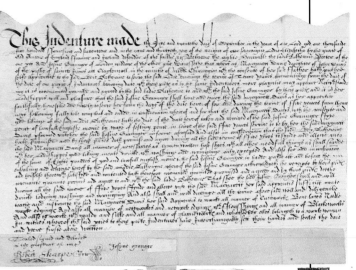

◁ **Servants bustle around a busy town.**
Servants in a town had more chance than those in the countryside to meet other servants, even to find a new employer, if they were unhappy with the one they had.

▷ **An apprentices' 'indenture'** (above right). This was a contract they had to sign: it said what they had to do and what their master had to do for them. Most apprentices were boys, but there were girl apprentices in trades such as laundry work. Apprentices worked for their master for seven years.

# THE HOME

**"Cottages are built with earth walls, low thatched roofs, no floorboards, few walls inside and no glass in the windows," wrote a Tudor traveller visiting Cornwall in 1602. "There are few chimneys, just a hole to let the smoke out."**

The traveller, Richard Carew, was describing the homes of ordinary people living in the countryside. Most poor families had to crowd together in one room. The poorest families even shared this room with their animals. But most families had a room separate from the animals, with a loft-like room above, used for storing food and sometimes sleeping in. These families did not have servants, but could still have relatives living with them.

△ **Inside the house of a poor farmer.** The main room is dark and gloomy. A wooden ladder leads to an upper floor.

◁ **A village home from a Flemish calendar made in 1520.** Houses in England would have been similar. Village houses were built from a wood frame filled with wattle (woven sticks) and daub (mud). Only the church and maybe the house of the most important person in the village would have been built from stone.

The homes of poor families may not have changed much in Tudor times. But many homes did change. Some wealthy farmers and merchants rebuilt their homes to make them more comfortable, more spacious and more private. These homes had glass windows, chimneys (to take away smoke from the fires) and more goods and furniture, too.

As for the rich, many of them also rebuilt family homes. They built grand houses, with lots of big windows (glass was expensive, so this showed they were rich) and grand gardens, beautifully laid out. The new homes were very big – everyone had lots of space.

△ **The Old Palace at Hatfield House,** Hertfordshire. Here, as a princess, Elizabeth I had been kept captive for several years by her sister, Mary Tudor. Nearby stands the newer grand house built for Robert Cecil, one of Elizabeth I's most important ministers.

# FAMILY OUTINGS

**People did not often go on family outings in Tudor times. However, once or twice a year the family might visit friends or relatives in another part of the country. And there were some events most family members might go to, if they could afford it.**

In Tudor times people did not get long holidays from work, to go away from home. But they did get days off. Most of these were on 'holy days', to celebrate religious festivals or saints' days. On these days everyone in the family could join the celebrations in the streets, and eat drink and dance the day away. Some holy days had entertainments or special plays that were performed each year. On St George's Day, many villages acted out St George fighting a dragon.

▽ **A peasant wedding in a village.** This picture was painted by Dutch artist Pieter Bruegel in 1568. In an English village, a wedding would have been as much of a focus for celebration by the villagers as by the family itself. Here, the bride is sitting in the middle of the long table, in front of the decorated wall-cloth.

People could also go on outings on their days off work. They could not travel far, so might only go as far as the next town or village. There was more to do in big cities. London was the only place that had permanent theatres and daily performances of plays. But travelling actors visited many places, where they performed in inns, private houses, barns or on stages made from the boards of their carts. Most people could go on picnics or rowing on the river. Going to hear a visiting preacher on a Sunday was a popular outing!

◁ **A family visits a Tudor theatre.** Only London had theatres built specially to watch plays. Very young children did not go to the theatre. But older ones did, especially apprentices. A family with older children might go to a carefully selected play as a treat.

▽ **Children played all sorts of games.** One of these boys is about to go outside to play tennis. His younger brother is 'riding' a hobby-horse – and even whipping it! Villages had a lot less choice of entertainments and events than a town. Village families had to make their own fun.

# THEN AND NOW

**How is today's family life different to Tudor times? The main differences are the size of families and how family life is organized.**

Tudor family households were much larger than most families are now. This is partly because there would have been servants and relatives living with the family, but also because they had more children.

Roles for women and men were more strictly defined in Tudor times. Married women ran their home and looked after the children. They did not go out to work. As soon as a woman married, anything she owned became the property of her husband. Children of all families, rich and poor alike, often went to live in other households from about the age of 12 onwards, either to work or to learn manners. Most children did not go to school, and started work as teenagers.

△ **Tudor people dressed** in far more complicated clothes than people do now.

▷ **The Tudor Family**
Here is a typical Tudor family. The father is a merchant aged 40. The mother is aged 36. There are three daughters, aged 15, 11 and 3 months, and three sons, aged 6, 4 and 2. They have two apprentices and two servants who work for them. They live in a house near warehouses, where the merchant stores his goods.
• Tudor families had about six children.
• Tudor adults lived to about 40 years of age.
• Most Tudor families had relatives living with them.
• Tudor families did not have healthcare or sanitation provided.

• Most Tudor families were Christian. They went to church at least every Sunday, as well as studying the Bible at home regularly.
• Most Tudor homes, even those of the well off, had bare floors. People didn't have many possessions or much furniture and privacy.

▷ **The Modern Family**
Here is a typical modern family. The father is a teacher aged 38. The mother, aged 37, helps run the local playschool. They have two children, a son aged 2 and a daughter 1 month old. They live on a housing estate near the school. The house has a garden. A lady comes to clean the house once a week. The mother and father share the shopping and housework.
• Modern families have about two children.
• Adults now live to about 90 years of age.
• Most modern families do not have relatives or household staff living with them.

• Most modern families have healthcare and sanitation provided.
• Modern families have a wide range of religious beliefs and practices.
• Most modern homes have more possessions, including luxury goods, and private space than their Tudor counterparts would have done.

# GLOSSARY

**abandoned** left to look after oneself.

**antiseptics** something that stops bacteria breeding, so keeps things clean.

**apprentice** someone who agrees to work with a master for a number of years to learn his trade, like baking.

**baby walker** a frame on wheels that keeps a baby upright when it is learning to walk.

**beggars** people with no jobs or money, who had to ask other people for money, food or shelter to live.

**breeches** trousers that reach to about the knee.

**confirmed** confirmation is a religious ceremony in the Christian Church. When children are confirmed they say that they understand and will do their duty as good Christians.

**court** the monarch and the people who lived and worked with the monarch.

**cousin** the children of your uncles and aunts or other close relatives.

**dairy** a place where cows are milked and where their milk is stored or made into butter, cream and cheese.

**divorce** legally ending a marriage.

**duty** something a person is supposed to do.

**frocks** dresses.

**gleaning** collect up the bits of corn that have been missed by the harvesters.

**heir** person who inherits the land and other possessions of a dead person.

**hobby horse** a carved horse's head on a stick, that children can pretend to ride.

**household** everyone living in the same house.

**manager** someone who runs a business or lands for the person who owns them.

**merchant** someone who sells things made or grown by other people.

**monarch** a king or queen.

**nephew** the son of a person's brother.

**noble** from one of the rich and important families in the country. Nobles usually had a title, like Duke of York.

**noblewoman** a female noble (see noble).

**orphan** a child whose parents are both dead.

**peasant** poor farm worker.

**preacher** a Christian clergyman or priest.

**Psalms** part of the Christian Bible.

**ruffs** frilled collars that stick out around the neck.

**rule** run the country.

**sack** to turn someone out of a job; to make them redundant.

**saint's day** a religious day celebrating something that happened in the life of a saint, a person that the Christian Church thinks is especially holy.

**sanitation** providing drains, sewers and running water, as well as taking away rubbish.

**swaddled** wrapped tightly in long strips of cloth with arms and legs straight down.

**tavern** a place that sells food and drink to other people.

**thatched** roofed with straw or reeds.

**ward** a child with no living parents (or whose parents the government distrusts) who is brought up by another family. People were usually only made wards if they came from rich, noble families.

**widows** women whose husbands have died.

## TIMECHART

**1485** Henry Tudor beats Richard III at the Battle of Bosworth. He becomes King Henry VII and the Tudor period begins.

**1509** Henry VII dies. His son, Henry, becomes King Henry VIII.

**1531** Henry VIII begins to change the religion of England from Catholic to Protestant (both are Christian religions). One reason is that he wants a divorce (from his first wife, Catherine, who had a daughter by him, Mary). The Head of the Catholic Church, the Pope, will not give him one, because divorce is not allowed in the Catholic religion. Only the Pope can grant a divorce, and only under very special circumstances.

**1533** Henry gets his divorce from the new Church and remarries. His new wife, Anne, has one daughter, Elizabeth.

**1536** Henry executes Anne. He marries his third wife, Jane, who has a son, Edward, but dies. Henry marries three more times, but has no more children.

**1547** Henry VIII dies. His son, Edward, becomes King Edward VI.

**1553** Edward VI dies. He names his cousin, Lady Jane Grey, as queen. But Edward's sister, Mary, takes over, and becomes Queen Mary I.

**1558** Mary dies. Her sister, Elizabeth, becomes Queen Elizabeth I.

**1603** Elizabeth I dies. James VI of Scotland becomes James I of England. The Stuart period begins.

# INDEX